Living in a Biome

Life in a Pond

by Carol K. Lindeen

Consulting Editor: Gail Saunders-Smith, Ph.D.

Consultant: Sandra Mather, Professor Emerita
Department of Geology and Astronomy, West Chester University
West Chester, Pennsylvania

Capstone
press

Mankato, Minnesota

Pebble Plus is published by Capstone Press
151 Good Counsel Drive, P.O. Box 669, Mankato, Minnesota 56002
http://www.capstone-press.com

1 2 3 4 5 6 08 07 06 05 04 03

Library of Congress Cataloging-in-Publication Data
Lindeen, Carol K., 1976–
    Life in a pond / by Carol K. Lindeen.
    v. cm.—(Pebble plus: Living in a biome)
    Includes bibliographical references (p. 23) and index.
    Contents: What ponds are—Pond animals—Pond plants—Living together.
    ISBN 0-7368-2101-5 (hardcover)
    1. Pond animals—Juvenile literature. 2. Pond plants—Juvenile literature.
[1. Pond animals. 2. Pond plants.] I. Title. II. Series.
    QH98 .L56 2004
    578.763'6--dc21   2002155668

Editorial Credits
Martha E. H. Rustad, editor; Kia Adams, designer and illustrator; Juliette Peters, cover production designer; Kelly Garvin, photo researcher;
    Eric Kudalis, product planning editor

Photo Credits
Ann & Rob Simpson, 16–17
Bruce Coleman Inc./Bob & Clara Calhoun, 4–5
Dwight R. Kuhn, cover, 20–21
Joe McDonald, 6–7, 12–13
Robert McCaw, 1, 10–11, 14–15
Tom Stack & Associates/Brian Parker, 8–9, Doug Sokell, 18–19

Note to Parents and Teachers

The Living in a Biome series supports national science standards related to life science. This book describes and illustrates animal and plant life in ponds . The photographs support early readers in understanding the text. This book also introduces early readers to subject-specific vocabulary words, which are defined in the Glossary section. Early readers may need assistance to read some words and to use the Table of Contents, Glossary, Read More, Internet Sites, and Index/Word List sections of the book.

Word Count: 147
Early-Intervention Level: 13

Table of Contents

What Are Ponds?

A pond is a small body
of still, shallow water.

Ponds are found in many parts of the world. Ponds form in forests, on farms, and in cities. Ponds are smaller than lakes.

Pond Animals

Many kinds of fish swim
in a pond. Fish breathe
through gills.

Ducks swim in the water.
They eat insects. Ducks
also dive underwater
to look for food.

Frogs kick and swim in the
water. Frogs eat insects.

Pond Plants

Water lilies grow in ponds.
Their leaves float on the
water. Their flowers bloom.

Cattails grow in ponds.
A cattail is a plant with a
fuzzy, brown tip. The tip
looks like a cat's tail.

Sunlight shines through shallow pond water. Sunlight reaches plants that grow on the bottom of the pond.

Living Together

Many plants and animals live
together in ponds. Animals
find food in ponds. Plants
need pond water to grow.
Ponds are full of life.

Glossary

gills—openings on the sides of a fish's head; fish breathe through gills.

insect—a small animal with a hard outer shell, three body sections, six legs, and two antennas; most insects have two or four wings.

lake—a large body of water with land on all sides

shallow—not deep; most ponds are shallow enough for sunlight to reach the bottom.

still—quiet, calm, or without motion

Read More

Galko, Francine. *Pond Animals.* Animals in Their Habitats. Chicago: Heinemann Library, 2003.

Halfmann, Janet. *Life in a Pond.* LifeViews. Mankato, Minn.: Creative Education, 2000.

Oliver, Clare. *Life in a Pond.* Microhabitats. Austin, Texas: Raintree Steck-Vaughn, 2002.

Internet Sites

Do you want to find out more about ponds?
Let FactHound, our fact-finding hound dog, do the research for you.

Here's how:

1) Visit *http://www.facthound.com*

2) Type in the **Book ID** number: **0736821015**

3) Click on **FETCH IT**.

FactHound will fetch Internet sites picked by our editors just for you!

Index/Word List